WYRD ENGLAND

Lakshmi Gill is a writer, artist, and educator with accumulated awards, grants, publications, exhibits, archived sound recordings, translations, and work used in secondary and university curriculum and international research. Lakshmi has published extensively in Canadian and world literature. She is one of the two women poets (along with Dorothy Livesay) who founded the League of Canadian Poets in 1966. A Punjabi Sikh/Spanish-Filipina writer, she lives on Burnaby Mountain in British Columbia. Current member of The Writers' Union of Canada.

Also by AUTHOR

Reconfigured Space (Mitchell Press, 2024)

On the Lanai (Miriam College of Family Authors, 2014)

With You (Sacred Heart Press, 2006)

Returning the Empties (TSAR Publications, 1998)

The Third Infinitive (TSAR Publications, 1993)

Gathered Seasons (League of Canadian Poets, 1983)

Novena to St. Jude Thaddeus (Fiddlehead Press, 1979)

First Clearing (Estaniel Press, 1972)

Mind Walls (Fiddlehead Press, 1970)

During Rain I Plant Chrysanthemums (Ryerson Press, 1966)

Rape of the Spirit (Colcol Press, 1962)

CONTENTS

PART ONE   7

PART TWO   25

PART THREE   40

ACKNOWLEDGEMENTS   55

© 2025, Lakshmi Gill. All rights reserved; no part of this book may be reproduced by any means without the publisher's permission.

ISBN: 978-1-916938-86-1

The author has asserted their right to be identified as the author of this Work in accordance with the Copyright, Designs and Patents Act 1988

Cover designed by Aaron Kent

Cover image: © Ekaterina Lanbina / Adobe Stock

Edited and Typeset by Aaron Kent

Broken Sleep Books Ltd
PO BOX 102
Llandysul
SA44 9BG

Wyrd England

Lakshmi Gill

Broken Sleep Books

PART ONE

Or own that truly here is home.
This is the worm-seed, fully known.
Inglond, Engelond: listen to the wind
around the word. No other sound.

This is the heart so full it leaps
in whorly palpitations, crosses boundaries
of graveyards and gardenbeds
joy o joys of human compost.

The wind around the word a host
of bardic ghosts, these Englyssh dead
in the soil, in the sands, in the seas,
these glorious bones, like dust that seeps

through every crack. Holy ground
trembles with their breath, Arthur-cold
exhumed again for country and for throne
but now, for loan, to stir this wintry loam.

Amidst the skeletons of stones, they speak
contre jour in muted tones, soft
rivulets of wash on wet-on-wet
sky of cobalt blue, ultramarine, these
coloured shadows, mirrored, overlaid,
bleed into each other, run to shade;
tidemarks of hues flow accidentally
chattering through my open window.

There they are: silhouettes illuminated
clearly, dull skylight behind them.
Onto me, dark object, they bring the world
wound round their heads like turbans,
whirl round and round my ring of walls
where I, enclosed, seek sleep in Wool
Britannia, which their icy knives cut
short, compel me to riotous decay.

Here in number 25, Arctic Parade,
two-storeys high, stone row houses,
beside mine to the left empty,
the right two occupied. Across
our thumbnail hovels, gravel for cars,
should we have them, and an island,
grassless, brown, defending us
from traffic winding down
grand Great Horton Road.

We have no gardens. None in front,
none back. One thorn, aslant,
atop the hill where the Road bends
guards us like the Rood of time.

But this grievance matters not
for here in bed my vision's strewn
hellebores, wintersweet, aconites,
frost hardy viburnum, crocuses
whose arms open to the skies---
here in my Mungrell Garden drifts

of poets scent the cloyed air,
shower me with misty lavender.
Infilled with heraldic earths
my intertwisted knot identifies
I, too, from blood and gore was wrenched,
by Duty, Dross and Dung chained.

Over seeming wrong, genius triumphs
and all is well if well is full---
love, divinity, sweete Themmes,
sweet Angels, ye Nymphes of Mulla---

it matters not. An embarrassment of Poets
speak in the wind around Engleterre
interred with their bones that good
rising now for sweet revenge.

No more the evils evil men quarter,
distribute with a sweep, measure,
to infants' lips. Caesar's angel run through.
The envious rent. The honourable dishonoured.

This spectral crowd crowded round
my doll-bed begins to glow as bright
as Turner's light, his Fighting Temeraire
hooked, pulled away from tow.

"It will not break! It will not die!"
(So they proclaim, a little loud,
a wintry blast; my neighbours will complain.
I implore, less shouting please, you Inglis hoar.)

Ba blah ba blah ba blah ba blah
His Worth in Words drones on
o'er crags and dales and glens and close
he lulls and soothes me to repose.

But sleep is gone. How easily love comes
to him whose Sister, Wife, and Friend (s)
do tend. How so loved can so loving so
imagine love in hills and daffodils.

His orange sky cries 'I' and 'I'
to evening his dappled day descends
borrowing the Gita's peace-surpassing-all-
understanding collected into English soil.

But here I am, not so magnificent.
A child of India cloaked in British mist
my own peace compromised and spent
assimilated by the laureate.

It makes no sense. "You loved him once," says C.
restless in Malta. It must be age, then,
annoys me now. Grow up, I say, grow up.
"What triggered this dissent?"

On hearing the justification
of first affections out of this Poet's labour
truth perished, twisted by master power.
The noisy years Silenced in one stroke.

It was then I could not hold it in.

Divinely forgiven, for only God
can forgive adulterers. All others
leave. Who are we to stone. Ha-ha.
Hail them with cheers and fountain days.
But lest we forget: in the upkeep
of aristocracies of Britaine Islands
is all civilizations' work
under a manufactured Indian sun.

The ceorl do toil, Sir, because they
are not free. The damaged compass,
the obsolete charts, the sloop low
on the waters all betide—nay—cry

"Havoc!"

It is the Picturesque gone mad. A people
in the margins like baboons illuminated
by Holy Manuscripts, framed in the light
of His Rude Holiness. It boggles my mind.

Don't say tradition. In Brighton Pavilion
we saw the loot first hand. We paid
(doubly) for the piracy those licensed
privateers extracted not just too long ago.

In memory's time. We do still remember.
That was my father's. And that. And that.

And that. And that. And that.
How can you look me in the eye?

"Oy!" clamour my dead bards in unison
some their harness clanking, chain mail rattling.
Old Ralegh there, head in hand, shouting "Fie!"
"Treason!" Loyal to the last. Just in case.

"Stand fast!" "Ho!" "Watch what you say, boyo!"
The little plagiarist whose own Wales's
visit ordered his universe pins me
with his poisoned dart. "Think we,

like some weak Prince, the Eternal Cause
prone for his fav'rites to reverse his laws?"
(like senile academics, he quotes himself
from yellowed sheets heroically coupled.)

The upkeep of arrogance imprisons
generations of multitudes
to servitude. Courtiers all.
A nation of servants. Doomed.

By all reason, wrong. Father to son
this legacy. Hereditary Right
uproots the rights of Everyman.
Shite. Let them clean their own toilet.

You cruddy Londoners, lewd ass-kissers,
you most obedient, humble servants

to Lords, Dukes, and Royal Dogs at Kew---
how else to publish? Whoring for poetry.

"Hold on," crabby George from Suffolk whispers.
"Though Belvoir Vale was rich and proud,
I suffered there as much as grimy Peter
in the marsh." "We cared, we cared."

"The greatest benefits for the greatest number."
"Not just for the few, the happy few."
"Have you no wit for irony? See not Sappho
the bohemian Lady much hounded?

"There high-mettled Atossa, fanny Sporus,
Namby Pamby, King of the Dunces---"
Yes, yes point made. It was a cruel age.
Treacherous, vicious, mean, back-stabbing,

double-dealing--- "Yes, yes, your point?"
Conspiracies go on. George will have his mistresses
but no other Caroline. Let's drink deeper.
With Alfred: was there a tiger in the grass?

If so, then say tradition. For that's the past
hallowed, sanctified in abbey arches,
grand halls, great church, cloister court.
What I, myself, would give for those fresh days.

Young England! Before the Dissolution.
When sacral bells rang out in Cistercian chapel,

Dominican vestry, Franciscan chancel,
Cluniac nave, Augustinian grange.
Younger Breatan! Before the Norman invasion.
Before Agricola and Caledonia.
To crannogs, brochs, duns,
souterrains, wheelhouses, and pents.

To the Ridiculous Sublime! Youngest still
at Lussa Wood, of rocks and middens;
at Skera Brae, of stone-hearths, cairns.
To gestation in the womb.

How much farther in one's youth can aged go?
Child fathering the man, indeed. Let Man stand.
Put aside the things of childhood. Take up his duty,
defend the land, protect the people.

I stood in London and saw a new century
blast the watery wall. Albion ascending.
Trident to the fore piercing the fog.
The loom of her land a bold beacon.
Europe shipwrecked on her shores,
salvaged. Beached here the world
from white Dover to raw Bristol, sleepy Penzance
to hoary Berwick-upon-Tweed, all ports open,
deluged with the flood of humanity.

In this island ark I heard the voices
of earth's commons, godless and godfilled,
honeyed and horrid, sad and saved,

and all, believing. A song of praise,
an alleluia, thanks be to True Home,
when, expatriated, the soldier, sailor,
merchant, governor, idler, adventurer,
sat in some forsaken hole and drank swill
groaning, "Oh, to be there!" Lord, help us.

The colonials bemoaned their existence,
the heat, the dust, the bloodied soil. God
help us. Oh, to be there with April rose
bloom, the winter chills shook off, the sun
gentle in a cloudless sky. There'll be a breeze
breathing through trees: beloved elm, yew,
ash, oak, beeches in the garden.
And in the air, slight scent of hyacinths.

Soft, soft England. Woolly.
Shepherded. Chosen. If Eden had been,
here Eden now. I stood in London
and saw the parting of the sea, the coming
of the people. Sinful, they came for salvation.
Hungry, they came to be fed. Prodigal,
they came to be housed again and safely.
Home, they are, to stay. Lord, help us.
Lord, help us. All to be forgiven.

"Listen, woman," the Blind Poet speaks in mid-stream.
"I said where were you when English brains
were handed out. Standing around?" Hey,
we also serve, we who stand and wait.

In fact, that's what we do: stand, wait and serve.
And now we'll serve no more. "Hurray!
cries out the Lame Poet. "Rhyme on our names,
but wisely hide your own." To which the BP turns,

"What are you on about? No Englishman you, you
continental lout. We didn't ride in your cortege.
Your bones we laid not in the Abbey. Go back to
Missolonghi." "Alack. The hurting never stops.

Why, think you, was I abroad? This island
horde my being chased away. To the ground.
To the very tunnel of the underground. To flee
and never to return was all that was left for me."

"You promised, I recall, in an epistle
to a friend, to whine no more. How typical.
Your kind do go on and on. Thank God
you all died young. And foolishly, I add."

"To die for Liberty---foolish?" The LP gasps.
"Then Fool was He who freed us from sin Original,
from Roman bondage, from false kings,
despots, tyrants; do recall my anti-Southeys."

All empires *have* expired, say I to calm him.
Your George was judged less viciously
by history. You really, truly wasted your venom.
British North Americans were British.

It was secession, not revolution.
Another civil war, fraternal confrontation.
The paranoia of one against the other.
Nothing more. All else was histrionics.

"Brother in brother's blood must bathe, rivers of death!"
Full of wrath & curse & rage, the Maddend Poet
trembling in the dark, furious in the shade,
dashes lightning at our astonished faces.

Undaunted, I speak on, like some hiker
who chances on a lunatic with tourettes
chastising himself in his father's voice
yelling sporadically—"I'm going to beat you! Idiot!"

And French complicity. Let's not forget our
ancestral enemy. But for your George all
Europe would be Gallic. "Instead, Germanic."
One hundred years of peace. True Victory.

"Ancestral enemy indeed. Transported
violence, you mean. The pirate Duke's
quarrel with his French king brought
to our land. Personal made national.

From that Normandy, debauched
with anarchy, the Bastard carried
his hatred, his struggles, his magnates
infesting us with his battles."

"If truth be told   'tis older thole
Finn and Hildeburh   harrowed in Friesland
lamenting the loss   of her son and Hnaef,
brother so brave.   Bodies blazed.

Hengest hid   wrath and rage
till time was ripe   revenge to take.
Then Finn was slain   silenced forever
Hildeburh and plunder back to Daneland kin."

"Spain, it was, not France. This endris countrie
plied the seas, makeless methinks
lowsit weir on civilised men, temit their coffers,
burned their firth, plagued their hussies."

"Let Liberty, the charter'd right of Englishmen
won by our fathers in many a glorious field,
enerve my soldiers," shrieks the MP
startling us again, diffusing the medieval sage.

"'Tis France, mark well my words, those ravening
wolves infest our English seas. But Liberty
shall stand upon Albion's cliffs. Our sons
shall rule the sea's empire." I'd settle for self-rule.

He passes round the death-cup that we
as one in Horror disdain. "We're dead,"
they cry in unison. "Not so!" He thunders.
"Not dead enough till you've seen the Abyss.

My Divine Vision! My Religion! My Giants!
My Emanations! My Albion-Jerusalem!
There I sat in fiery London, setting America free.
My Lamb of God! My English Child!

Jerusalem, thy Sister calls! You Patriarch David.
The Tree of Mystery saves the little Flock
from Hill to Hill from the Oppressors that mock
the Labourer's limbs. Limbs that burn in the Furnace,

in Stones of Fire. Die a True Death, you Scops.
Kill the memory of Sin. Man must have the Religion
of Jesus. Enough of your glorious Satans.
(at which point the BM and the LM sneer and scoff)

Acquit not your Alexanders and Fredericks,
your Whores of Wars, your Edward Henry Elizabeth
James Charles William George. Nobles who taxed
nations into Desolation. England! Awake!"

Panting, the MP wraps his fury in his linens
and we, the ravished, exchange glances.
"Uh, done is he?" The wordsmith mutters,
gloomy he's been outblah'd, the inner

Grain of Sand outspacing his lofty mountains.
"Rather it's those Germanic Nouns in Capitals
disturb my little train of reason. Too big,
I daresay. They lose their sting."

"Hear, hear," the LP nods. "Too Enthusiastic.
No soft Italianates and points well made
sans repetition." "Hmm," the BP shudders.
"And he says I was his mentor?"

So where was he, I laugh, when your so-called
English brains were handed out? "Methinks
he queued twice and over and got the lot."
"Or scattered the bits from Highgate to Harrow."

The MP's red eyes blaze. We cower.
Thank God the Son of Morning rose, redeeming
me from more debate. The phantom bards disperse
not as they appeared, sullen and desolate,

but grumblingly, not melancholic now,
all testy and hot, troubled, promising
a return in 24 hours ere the cock would crow
again to disturb my sleep as visions will.

They cry: "Close, England! The enemy, within!"

I hie to my toilette, turn on the heat
for the shower. Freezing to gradual warming
the water washes out the Crazy Cold
whose God must go insane from listening
to their laments---"Och, aye, we will drain
our dearest veins."---"That Patron of Mankind
in Arms abroad defend."---Complain, complain.
My thoughts are all jumbled in my tangled hair.

Shampoo flows across my eyes when suddenly
my flesh tingles. There's someone here.
I wash away the riot of demons and marvel.

He leans, whiskey in hand, against the tiles
that wall my cubicle. An unseeing eye
(unseeing me but seeing his Adamic solitude)
shimmers at the cascading sheen. "Remember,"
he intones, "that day you stood in London."
Green light on glistening grass. It filled my sight.
Uncommon green England made common.
How could I forget? The Myth bought.
The Edengates breached. Paradise resurrected.
But how did you escape the morning?
He shrugs impatiently. "Death is dead. Means nothing.

Look, woman. We went before; we cast the kingdoms old.
All's done with the axe's edge upon the bleeding head.
Their powers circumscribed. Their gardens halved.
Where once a hundred gardeners, now down to two.
Would you deny them that, at least, the few
who will uphold their spirits? For like the falcon,
we, having killed, must search no more but perch.
We, victors, must sheathe the sword
and hang the corslet. If ever our vigilant
Commons summon us to oil the armour yet,
we'll stand this kingdom united and sung.

Our kings and queens and princes of Wales
however odd, intemperate, and spoiled, we must

possess. This is the English Myth, the Eden Myth,
the Garden inviolate. Those bowers of bliss,
sacred groves, orangeries, Caroline's serpentines,
Anne's oblong ponds, the Regent's cultivated
glades, greedy climbers sweet-smelling and secret---
now ours to enjoy. Rhododendrons for Tom.
What more to allay the stresses of office.
Tom walks the park where the Ansbach royal once said
stank of people. Stinking now, this freed landscape.

The world comes. It wants us to maintain
the Ancients of our days. Indwelling God
forever, once and future king unwavering."
The heady mixture of climate and discomfort
pushes our imagination up like weeds between
gravestones. Those American anglophiliacs,
I rejoin, methought came for tourist thatch
and Tudor quaint. Tintern guided textbooks.
Highland tales. Ossian illusions. Magic Playland.
Medieval Themepark. Twenty pounds admission.
I struggle with the increasing heat, lather, rinse.

"Why, you ask? It's comforting. Against the slaughter,
blood following blood, this pleasant land, this pleasure
ground, this artful ruin." Speaking of which,
shouldn't you have crumbled by now? Rosy Morne
has gone to shade. "I published posthumously.
Nature lies under poetic feet," he shrugs.
"So, in truth, the world's imagination runs
to the Fount. Hic jacet Arturus rex quondam

rexque futurus. Behold!" He swings his bottle
upward like his Cromwell, valorous,
indefatigable. "Behold! The healing drink!"

Then crashes. The shattered glass cut my skin
then fade like special effects in films.
I look around to check if any more dear
departed hangs in shower curtains. None espied,
I dress and quickly leave this floor of vanishings
and musings, run down the narrow stairs for fear
of late encounters and shy versifiers,
headlong to the ground floor of my kitchen
with its faux-Greek marble linoleum,
stone cold walls, pale and shivery, when,
up above, his voice shouts, "The heat. Save energy!"

So up I run again and turn it off but keep
my eyes closed for I'm not bold. On kings I would
my pen keep sharpened but Poets: the rub.
They are scientists in the interstice. Between here and there
they lie in wait, ready to pounce on complacence,
push our conscience to action, remind us,
in their proliferation as rich as earth
regenerating season after season, as well as
in their repetition as nagging as prayer
voicing and revoicing the same devotion: the point.

"You ostrich in the sand, do I not your big butt see?
Pluck out your fetters, look at me!" This one
just won't go away. "To the Matter that inspired

this lay, this afterthought: why, think you,
should he care? Unmanned, ungunned, unsung.
No duty where Duty's been removed. How far does a duchy
go? O woe. The rent's reduced, what Gold
to purchase? This paltry life he must endure.
What tarnished wife must follow Glory. Glistering
in the withering sun let him, at least, be happy.
This is our English Grace. We're done beheading."

All is forgiven.

PART TWO

        In the kitchen
        at ten to ten
        by Old Ben

        I still sit
        eat my bit
        true dimwit

        no school today
        happy to say

        Saturday it is
        been up to piss

        ghosts all gone
        when

Scuffling in the corners
like mice in the floorboards
the Nobles jockey for room.

What?! Will these spectres
not quit? More crowded
in my hovel than Smart's head

where Cat Jeoffry creeps
and swims with jubilant
life. Now with one leap

into my tea, this best
of English Cats of Europe
sweeter in rest

his rat-bit throat
wet in leaves, purrs
in my cup-boat:

"God is benevolent."

"No more than We,"
one Noble shouts.
"We let you live."

Poor Jeoffry! I succour
for Christopher's sake,
one fellow inmate to another.

"What time is it?
Not even noon? Too early.
See you at 3."

Gone away. Like hares
with sudden appointments
hearing 'Tally Ho!' into their lairs.

Well, Dan Leno, sing us a ditty
from the Duchess of Piccadilly Circus' county
where Lord De No Oof and the Baron in the mansion
taught you Follow-the-Hounds and Corruption

oops, sorry, I meant to say Attend-the-Meet,
Buge-the-Bugle, Jump-the-Hedge, Unhorse-the-Seat,
---what infinite joys these games---Follow-the-Scent,
---to all our Lords and Ladies lent---
Take-It, Pip-Pip, To Horse! again, excuse,
the mind exerts beyond the hunter's muse.
These jollies they play for rabbit and fox
seem but exercises to kill the Rex.

>   Gone away, they, no hurry
>   to return. To tarry in bed
>   while the tenants scurry.

>   How sweet it is to lie
>   and lie and lie
>   and lie and lie and lie.

Meanwhile, in halls less baronial,
music, hooting, waggery, benders
fill men's, uh, Marie Lloyd, fill our ears
with railway clacks, the London fog,
the Piccadilly moan, the Euston giggle,
(We're told the Queen watched *Eastenders*.
We're in good company.) the people's voice.

It's a quarter ter four
And Jeerusalem's dead.
His missus and the youngsters
he loved but the donkey more.
For all that he fed

that devil still went under.
Rum in his hand, lump in his chest,
(un poco animato, ma teneramente)
he nusses my sympathies, doctors my head.
"'E 'ad a big 'eart, 'e was the best.
I gave 'im my grub, I gave 'im my bed.
What for? What for?
(tranquillo) Jeerusalem! Things turn to frost."

> "Quarter to 4?
> Where does time go?
> Lo! High tea."

(allegro moderato)
"Wot? I'm plain in me habits
and plain in me food.
'Arf a pint of ale, a pint and a narf
that's good enough. A barrel of beer
is not for the tip like corfee
and tea and cocoa and milk.
Shut up. Just give me my barf."

> "Scones, pastry,
> marmalade, O!
> Do pour!"

(passionata)
"Pickled onions, cabbage, termartoes,
cucumber, boiled beef, tripe,
baked sheep's heart, trotters,

(my mouth waters) radishes, hot meat pies.
Don't give me no fancy
asparagus, chaffinches, and jams.
Hungry, Joe? You bet I am!"

(allegretto)
"So you can fill your tummy
that's a larf. Ha ha.
Dinner's underneath your table
underneath the sky. Naughty,
naughty, can you pay the rent?
I can hear your children running
up and down the phantom stairs."

(tempo di valse)
"What about Trafalgar Square?
Be my roommate; I have room
to spare. We'll promenade
at breakfast, dinner and tea
with the swells and Clarence de Clares,
the selfish, the greedy who dwell
at the Metropole and the Cecil."

(moderato)
"And when a stranger in the street
asks you for the time, you take
your watch, say, here, look---
with one bound, out of your hand
into his. Wait a minute. Meet
his eye but you can't. (cough, cough)
Strange faces make you meek."

"You fool. That was Baron Hardup."
"A rent collector I've never seen."
"But daily walks in the Embankment!"
"Who knows who lurks behind high fences."
"We're all collectors against the ice."

Shy tramps in wet galoshes.

> The Dowager Duchess of Diddle
> goes "Bang! Go away with your fiddles.
> I will have my vittles!"

The curtain falls. The jingles
fade. The tingles
die.

More tea?

Cat Jeoffry, happily, stays.
Cherub Cat, protect me.
I fear these Nobles
more than fierce poesie.

"Pray, woman, iambic pentameter
if you please. Rhyme royal.
Heroic quatrain, maybe, or alexandrine,
that iambic hexameter
favoured by Spenser. Epic, if you can,
no mock. No meditative lyric.
No elegy. If sonnet, no Petrarchan

but Shakespearian, better yet, Spenserian.
No limerick. If ode, Pindaric.
If sestina, then double.
No peasant villanelle.
Well, another gracious Faerie Queene?"

Ah, to shew your auncestrie?
What peevish gealosie.
By soveraigne hand you were favoured:
land, sheep, castle, the laboured.
All intertwined your lofty crests
in crafty weave and marriage breasts
tight knots and plots and fortunes made
in th' Ocean mayne, in secret glade.
By God in heaven, you've been paid.

Duke Back-in-the-Tower roars,
"With our lives! Confiscated, attainted,
decimated, quartered, disembowelled.
Name it, we've paid indeed to party courts,
parliaments of devils and councils of realms."

That's what you get for fealty.
You pledged, you liegemen, your lives
for your king's wars: servitum debitum
for counties, towns, estates, and all
the peasants you could eat. You sold to the devil.
Grand servants. Where's the nobility?

"Our kings would reward one, impoverish
the other. Like God they would take
because they had given. We lived in fear,
albeit aristocratically. We had to give
good servitia debita." Whatever, Dude,
give it a title; you were servants, doomed.

"More importantly,
we think the rhyme scheme's off.
Not couplets. It's ababbcbcc."
Your toff
is far too silly.
Too decorative for me.
That fabulous Inventor
I cannot be.
I'm no Philosopher.
No Master.

"Now, in iambs hexametrically
and mingle the rhyme with allegory.
We'll yet get our family story
told."

"Yield, wench."

When surrounded by hefty swords,
'tis wise to feign acquiescence
and later on, away from lords,
to the Higher Lord clear conscience.
Nod and nod in meek obeisance.

How else survive royal purges,
the whims, the arrows, the nonsense,
the daggers, the pox, the urges?
Hold in the hot blood that surges.

"Not quite. Pentameter, pentameter.
Do keep trying; hard work will get you there.
Ti dum ti dum ti dum ti dum ti dum
Each day the rains do go, the rains do come.
But labour strong and plow that land for me
and graze my sheep for all eternity.
To you I pledge by king and country dear
your safety, turnip, and your precious beer
against the foes harrowing my curtain wall."

Note all the aforesaid in couplets all.
Let's just poor rich Edmund sleep it off.
He's had his share of troubles, too.
Sure, he had his poetry
shored against court intrigues
intricate wordplay
rhyme and riddles
to keep sane
in life's
strife.

I
need not
your favours.
No feudal vassal.

I toil for no man.
The air I breathe is free.
I'll gather from all poets
their mildewed attic-words
don their motley wild-pied apparel
inhabit their incorporeal wit.
Ah, the jumble, free-for-all, music hall Great Fall.

The Nobles rhubarb rhubarb
in my narrow kitchen, stuffed
like sausage bulging in its skin.
"Turn the damned heat on,"
Earl Falsetto bellows. "Central
heating's been invented."
What need of warmth for shades? I chide.
"Oh, we're not dead yet, lass,
as long as kings walk about the land
and people line the barriers, cheer them on.
We were born to keep them ever hopping---

the one to watch where trodding, the other
leashed. Since good William
we were there, black thorn on his side---
or knife or damocletian sword,
what-have-you. Normans, yes, but,
with native brood with princess Eadgyth.
We're stock. You're stuck.
You can't undo, however bloody, History."
"I beg to differ. We only butchered sheep."
"This is a tough neighbourhood.
I can't walk around without my friends."

"Do go. It's warmer outside than here."
Can't. It's on automatic: 5:28 to 8 p.m.
I'm on a smaller budget called hand-to-mouth.
Here's a jumper, old Scottish-Anglo-Norman
knit. By sair sanct, no less. Holy Kingdom,
David on this side of the Bible sanctioned.
Dispenser of sacred tenure. Anointer of Crowns.
Peacemaker of promises, north of the Tyne.
Landholder paragon. Peer paramount.

"Deil take thee, Lizzie! May a livin' plague
befall thee ere another word. Owre Scotland rings.
Let's set the Record straight."
Ok, ok, here have a wee drap of guid auld
Scotch Drink but please, no brogue.
It hurts my head. Here, glass o' whisky
to fill your poor verses as did the bard
o' plays and pranks at ither's arses.

"The English language I have mastered. Can't say
the other way around for you, you one-tongued wight.
Too arrogant to learn. Rather force us.
Of compromises the tale's been told.
We're not all to our claymores rise.
So, there we were in the Competition
after the Maid died in transition. No heir.
The Guardians chose Balliol over Bruce
with Edward's intervention. But here, I pause.
The blood boils."

While you compose, I'll bake more scones.
What is it about Scottish songs that make
me eat and drink where English only tea?
The standing pool? The dyke?
Be 't water-brose or muslin-kail
(John Barleycorn, the king o' grain)
this scanty meal my body claims.
I sing, I dance, I rhyme away,
Infernal fog and bitter winds no sway.

As smells of hearth spread through the house,
the Nobles cluster round the Argyll duke
like lean to fat. Here's something more to take.
"Contained, are you? No boiling over?
Emotions reined, passions averted?
Can't have you leaping on the table
(Ikea, this, no solid oak, so breakable.)"
Excuse me, some of us must earn our living.
Not for us Seynt Albons.
Damirabilis detestabilisque depraedatio.

"Go on, then, fellow lord. No Paramount,
no Overlordship, but worthy affinity."
"Edward in collusion with a Parliament
in his pocket, hence to Berwick
for Balliol. And Balliol forced to fealty
and King at Scone a progress made"
"---Delicious, these, by the way."
I raise my brows. The Scot's ballistic.

"Damn you, Sir. That streak drawn by Nature
there still down your back. Humiliation.
How good you are at it. Superior.
Our Stone of Destiny you thieved, meant
to shame us. This is your legacy."
My one other Ikea chair breaks in two.
A clatter of arms sounds the alarum.
By God! The Eternal Feud! Here yet again
the fractured families. Cousin to in-laws.
Half-brother to grandson. The Clash of Names.
Revenge and retribution. Massacre and treachery.

Quarrel, retaliation, murder, outrage, savagery.
Raid and campaign. Treaty and betrayal.
Good grief! It hurts the head.
Nothing is forgotten. Nothing is forgiven.
All remembered. All shriven.
Where, I ask, are the rank and file?
Slaughtered with the gentles, gang pressed
and bought for the price of root veggies.
From William then to William now.

Jeerusalem's dead. God help us.
Just give us our bread.

"Well," they turn to me, all red,
"We see we're not appreciated.
We're off, then, you nothing teacher fool
of some nothing Yorkshire school."

They cry: "A Charles! A Charles! The invaders, within!"

Poof!
At last. The quiet.

I wash dishes.

The Rat Inspector comes today.
Go, Cat Jeoffry. He's got poison.
The infestation is greater than your ken.

Smells of incense mingled with perfume
fill the air. Swish of damask, gold-inlaid,
touch my ankle. What's this? A mitre.
The Archbishop Marquess fades in.

The dead just won't stay dead. Least
of all the Church. "Ahem," he clears
his throat. "As to the Matter that inspired
this lay, this afterthought." Oh, that.

"Yes, it *is* all personal. The country runs
through Our Person. Basis of Our Bond:
the Grand Pyramid Scheme.
Head Crown, gut Lords, feet retainers.
Our good lordship feed the gentry.
Mediocres lust to be gentles. Earls lust to be kings.
Cut off a part, everything collapses.
We must uphold. Else lose our holdings."

Would not a pilgrimage of penitence
to Jerusalem have been in order? A monarch's
honour? "Too hard. My blessings suffice.
Who cares? Who really cares? Peasants
are trampled, their towns plundered
to suit Our Power. There can be no more
risings when we've ground them low and neat.
Despondent, they become indifferent.
Ahem. Kiss my ring?"
Sod off, Your Holiness.

PART THREE

From the sink, I turn
and here's the cellar door.
Down the rough stairs I go,
skitterish. Don't wish to tumble.
No one would ever find my corpse.
Damp to damp, decay.
The worm inside to die of cold
and ague. All living, mold.
Grow old. Grow old.

There, my removal boxes
from Asda stacked in a corner
(just two months ago prim, proper,
sturdy) now gone slimy
faster than you can say
a Northern sentence.

Two months ago and still
I nod and smile. Yesterday,
the pastoral counsellor
counselled me for twenty minutes
in gibberish, kind soul, God bless him.

Fumbling for the switch, I view
the devastation. Worse
than Yorkshire harried by William
massacring across the Pennines
littering the highways with rotting corpses.

Whatever wars kings will invent
nothing is grander than Nature's waste.
This must be hell. Not fire and brimstone.
Fake as the stage, those pulpit images.

My leichenhauser, my cellar
where everything I store putrifies:
this is hell. Smell the ammonia,
the acid in the air. White crumbly bits
on torn leather seats. Grave wax
on old files. Papers decomposed.
The mummy suitcase sags, reunited
with the soil. All my dead are buried
in my koimeterion, deep within my home.
My dress transforms to black silk crepe,
flat, sheenless, jet.

"Hello? Is anyone there?"
Out of the depths. Kayleigh? Sarah? Jane?
Ginger-haired Sean? Innocent Ian?
What goes? Didn't I see you in Third Period?

"Miss! Here to lay out more traps
as if we weren't over-trapped?" The Rat
Inspector comes today, I say, surprised.
One can never have enough. They so
proliferate.

"Misery does. That's what misery does."
"Proliferation and putrefaction."

"Bulge in the coffin." "In the frozen bilge."
"Feel the moisture creep."

Waves of just before-the-bell wash over
me. Headmistress tells us: be extra kind
to James. His mum's in jail. Last year,
his da's suicide destroyed her, as if she
couldn't be destroyed again. Dear tiny James,
all doled out.

Now get out there and love them.

"Miss! For lack of to-do, we train these pets.
They jump for us, they clear the hedge.
Tricks and turns, hoops and fire-acts
to set your hair on edge. Would you like
to see a show?"

For lack of TV, they go nutter.
They can't afford it.
TV licensing fee paid quarterly
at ₤109 plus ₤1.25 each
so ₤28.50 per 3 months debited
from my account.

For this amount I see mock-Britain
stuck in the glory days of the 16th Century.
With amazing grace, the 17th and 18th are hid
shackled in irons in Caribbean and African suns;
the 19th is glimpsed for its redeeming Clapham.

The Big 5: Properties, Archaeology, The War,
Gardening, Wildlife. Then News, Architecture,
Games (cooking, children's, adults'),
Royal History, Competitions.

"Miss! You're not listening! Nobody
ever listens." Go on, then. Show me.
Once, I made the school's Dreaded Bully
sit beside me at my desk and write his
composition. The story went:

"I was 12 and I lived in Buttershaw.
One day I got to five minutes away
from school when these lads from another
asked me if I would lend them 25 p.
I said I need my money for dinner.
So, the lads said give me it or else.
I tried running but not fast enough.
They caught me and beat me up.
I didn't tell anyone for I was frightened.
The lads carried on taking my money
everyday until I was too scared to go.
My mom was thinking why. Eventually,
I told her and the police sorted it out.
But the lads kept on attacking my house
it was hell. We had enough so we moved
to Woodside, a flat in Bierley that flooded,
a flat in Allerton because grandma died,
Halifax which I didn't like, and then
I moved in with father because my mother

could not afford to feed seven kids
without any help."

Next, I saw him in detention
---a portable room we were locked in
(though I had a key in secret,
this being that day my duty).
"Look, Miss," he said, "there's a window.
It's all a farce. Open it. I won't jump out.
Want a cigarette?"

The rats make a pyramid. Sean, his toque
on as in class, sings the flourish.
Innocent Ian goads in the wings
stage-frightened Tommy to somersault.
Sarah hoots and hollers. Jane produces
her harmonica. Kayleigh flicks a lighter.

Ooh, can't have that. Breaking all the rules
now. Head of Year would yank her out,
send her home. Who's at home in Holmewood?
Brother James, 14, and Mum.
Dad lives with his wife, Ann,
and brother Liam, 4, two stepsisters
called Stephanie and Rachel, 13 and 10.
Mum's Pam; Dad's Stephen.
Best to keep her with me. First warning:
write name on board. Now, Kayleigh,
hand it over. Two big boys erupt into a fight
at the back. Bigger boy choking the other.

So angry. The children are so angry.
By the time I pry them loose, one has
red marks on his neck, passing out.
Can't do this. Year 8P1. I quit.

The professional rats focus me.
Painted backdrop: arbour under a dun,
cloudy sky. Tommy chewing the scenery.
There Athamas, Thunder god, locked
in embrace with Ino, she who makes
sinewy. And fair Nephele chances
on them in the Bower of Bliss.

Nephele the Spectre dark tears flowing across a ruined face
shuddering in horror at the holocaust of morality all that
decency touted English base of marriage vows gone!
Flown away and all that's left are the skeletal rags
of human flesh whose humanity is killed in the ovens
in one furtive act. And another even at the marriage bed.

Ino the Sinewy protests every Harlot was a Virgin once
in the Gates of Paradise all holy children of God pure innocence
all holy we are, all holy, Babe formed in pure Mould
no agony just comfort comfort comfort fall fall
into my Compassion, I am not Despair, I am ever Pity
& soft & listening board sounding the god's thunder.

Hera! The Spectre calls. Being of Pity & Compassion
even greater, you who vowed to uphold Vows eternal
when Loyalty meant something speak now and uphold.

Once and future Queen, Family first and foremost of this earth
to whom we turn to, our lives offered
our earnings shared for your comfort comfort comfort
that you will always be clothed in holiness & solitude
This is the day, this is the hour.

Hera the Upholder silent hitherto Now I will speak my mind
breaks silence & curses the Insult, My eternal vengeance
shall fall upon Athamas & his House! For she knows her Zeus
to be a philanderer royal eye-rover mistresses hidden
from her ever and ever from the beginning of their time
of Power. Who but she must have some standards
by which her Church insists their serfs must obey.

Delighting in cries & tears Nephele broadcasts on Mt. Laphystium
Hera's curse. Behold I will not be beheld and abhorred
the Virgin become Harlot by infidelity where nature
would have a Steadfast Wife be. Become fallen & monstrous
by cruelty & affliction & desert joy.

A Chorus of men of Boeotia with one voice say No to Hera
We fear Athamas more than you, he who feeds on Sacrifice
& Offering, he who thunders through our homes bolts & terrors
beyond imagining. O we fear him, god Athamas, he will break
our bones brittle from labour in his furnaces the anvil falls.

A Chorus of women of Boeotia with one voice say No to Hera
We love Ino, she's so English, quiet, grounded, not hysterical.
She knows when to hide when to appear like fog in London docks.
She's there always & forever persistent like the worm

in the sick rose, perpetual & undying, she is soil
Life living on consuming contrary to Almighty.
Moloch, her son, living it up in Jerusalem.

And Nephele goes underground tunneling into desecration
exiled from her crowded bed into chaotic nights
of desolation unloved pursued by Furies of jealousies & doubts
while Athamas perplexed by her wantonness & rejection
of his rights to unbridled passions roars at the Forge
triumphant with worshipped Ino as the Chorus behind masks
masking their afflictions stand in the darkening stage
waiting in fear for the threatening hammer that beats on
their submission.

Hera, defeated, sets her smile on her mouth the deadliest thing
rivaling the Skull grin deader than Death about to die
fixed tight by some surgeon clipped flesh nowhere else to go
this marvellous enigmatic public fused lips mock no more.

"Stop roaring, Tommy. The play's over."

"Miss!" (That's getting annoying.)
"Ta-da! Did you like it?"
My bum is withering into the rug.
Dreariness sets in.
The dungeon smells of all that's rotten.

Would I could bring you to Whitby.
Graves there have turned into gardens.
The churchyard trembles beneath tourists' boots.

Names are obliterated
now a communion of dead
consigned to some phantom heaven
overlooking a restless hill.

Darling children of rituals and distractions,
the darkling world is within.

The lead knocker, knocking, disperses
this decrepit mist into more nothing.
Slowly, I ascend steps, numbness chilling
my unholy soul touched by the unholy Tree.

My cellar door, sable gates, locking
out sunrises, light of lights,
hiding in the aborted sublime,
epics never to be, lives lost
how cold poetic feet how cold.

Spectator, turn actor or victim be
in this wretchedness. Partake of the play.
The pursuit of happiness is a royal task
deep in polo and parties, glitter and gifts,
spas and pets, champagne and cakes.
Treat yourself royally as royals do
wetshod in wine, the round of mansions
in winter and summer, autumn in This House,
spring in That, grand tours, sun resorts,
all taxing and daunting.

It's not easy. Cowards die depressed.
Bully yourself into going. Get your way
away from pain into pleasure. Fight
for the riches of heavens; leave these hells
flowing generation unto generation.

The buck will not come to you. You must empark.
Take up your balsam sword and twat at weeds
to let those tulips grow. And should it strike
some other heads, well, that's how it goes.
Or so our royals show. Yes, life triumphs, Shelley.

The Rat Inspector has come around to the back.
I open the kitchen door to his gloomy face.
Would that he had brought asphodel roots
and seeds, mint, myrtle, rosemary---
but no, in his mighty hand I see
black poplar in white cypress wood.
(I note, not dancing floorboards
Boer women used for their babies' coffins.)
Those damn rats. Now, it's personal.

No word passes between us. He strides in,
checks under the sink. Abased and useless,
I sit and wait. I think: they're gone, you know,
gone to the empty house adjoining this.
I hear the sound of castanets, heels tapping
on a table. Bright rats emigrate. Distance
gives perspective.

The rats who bide are timid. They prefer
the monopoly, the one-man show. They are hid.
But give them glitter and glow occasionally
and they'll come out to cheer then shuffle
back to their dreary corners. *Wha sae base
as be a slave*? Ah, this trade of hell.

And here they are, systematically paraded,
bagged. A frozen smile freezes over
the ministerial face. He twists the ties
that seal their fates.

> O Tommy go
> the pipes, the pipes are freezing
> from drain to drain and down the sewer-main.
> The winter's here and droopy snowdrops are budding.
> It's you, it's you must blow; I must remain.
>
> And don't come back
> though rains return on moor and fen
> or when the storms rage on in dale and glen.
> Sure, I'll be here forever wet and sodden
>
> O Tommy go, O Tommy go, I love you so!
>
> But if you come
> next winter when hell is freezing,
> I will be dead dead then, of course, I'd be.
> You'll see the barrow of my entombing
> and stand and say 'Shite, this could've been me.'

> And I'll hear your big boots heavy above me
> and all my stone will colder, trodden be.
> For you'll shout to the sky 'Ah, yes, she loved me."
> Then I'll sleep in peace for you won't come back to me.

We need the old to keep our youth
our flesh to please, our soul to soothe.
The curse of Memory sits on our brow
to keep the aged past an ever present now.

Thus, the worm-seed feeds. The land bleeds.

The promissory runes on white bones stake
the Future. The sleeping knights will awake.
Ring the bell, speak the incantation.
The waiting stones will dance again.

The future tense trembles in the tomb.
Past perfect will eject out of the encircling womb.
The language is completed to its doom.
Doom. This is the sound of the loom.

One better than Om. One sigh too far.
That grasping stretch collected O behind the bar.
In other climes, how easily thrown that O,
a seed to furrowed soil. We harvest what we sow.

The Rat Inspector grins at me as if to say
the days of noble Houses rushing off to war
beside their king are gone. Today

it's inconceivable to send the Ivory Tower
princes alongside soldiers. Just the poor
now, see? The hungry lured and baited.
Prop up the dead bodies of ancestral poison
and they'll follow behind the thinning line,
deluded by red, colour of sweet-smelling edam.
He is victorious. The conquered native conquering
all, like the bully, bullied once, bullies evermore.
The dark passage of the burial mound enthralls
and down to my cellar the invader goes.

You expect the other to do the decent thing
(as you would). Die (you think), you're evil.
Die on your own. Let go! But no.
Indecent, they will cling. An enforcer
must be sent. So there good governaunce
ensures reductions, eradication.

He emerges from the Otherworld a Hogboy,
head among ghosts, in his hands the faeries
dead dead dead.

They bled, they bled.
He leaves, the hero, until another day.

For there is no end to hallucinations.
The rats are here to stay.

The rats are here to stay. Round the twist.
The sinister land enratted. Made intimate.

Their droppings mark each gateway,
giant holed stones healing sick babies,
stone circles for dreams and sacrifices,
sun temples for rituals and stories.

Land of Magic! Gramarye!
How they fear you!
Each well, each spring, each tree reticulated.
Here on this rock, a tale inwoven;
in this forest, a Robin Hood; that dyke, a devil;
this hill, Gog. And all their chroniclers
are crossed: Geoffrey as invaluable
as Arthur and Merlin in Caerleon.

They pull the woolen blanket over their heads
against the rows of haunting portraits.
Guarding them, their geomythology.

ACKNOWLEDGEMENTS

Excerpt from 'Wyrd England,' *Prism International* (University of British Columbia), 49: 3 (Spring 2011): 50-51. ----four stanzas

beginning with
                        I stood in London and saw a new century

and ending with
                        Lord, help us. All to be forgiven.

LAY OUT YOUR UNREST

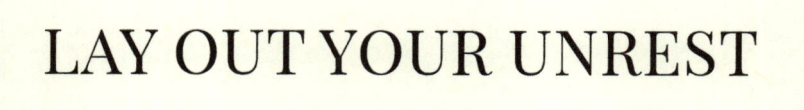

www.ingramcontent.com/pod-product-compliance
Ingram Content Group UK Ltd.
Pitfield, Milton Keynes, MK11 3LW, UK
UKHW031008070325
455963UK00004B/163